Buying & Selling the Souls of Our Children

A Closer Look at Pokémon

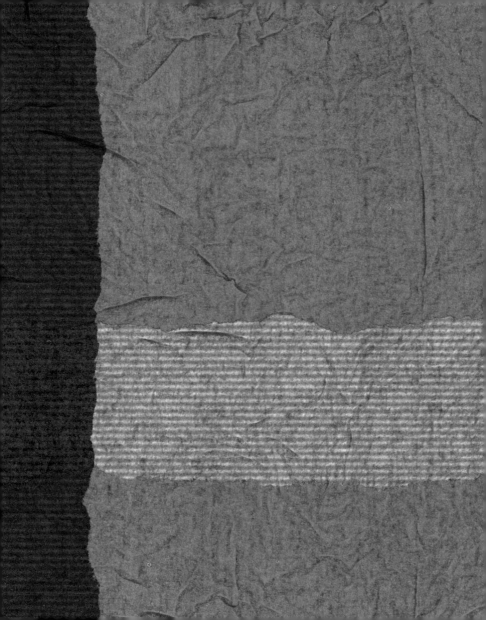

Endorsements

Many people are unaware of the spirits behind the role-playing phenomenon. John Paul Jackson has prayerfully researched this subject. Thank God for his discernment concerning holy and unholy influences. I highly recommend this book.

Wesley Campbell
Pastor, New Life Vineyard, Kelowna, Canada
and Executive Producer, *Praying the Bible* series

Buying & Selling the Souls of Our Children is a must! John Paul Jackson has sounded a clear, cutting-edge warning. I urge each of you to get this book into the hands of as many people as possible.

Bobby Conner
Founder, Demonstration of God's Power Ministry
Moravian Falls, North Carolina

John Paul Jackson has given us a timely book that will keep the prophetic generation that God is raising up from being seduced to the dark side. Read! Be warned! Be equipped!

Lou Engle
Author, *Digging the Wells of Revival*

With the skill of a Holy Ghost undercover agent, John Paul Jackson lifts the skirts on one of the most deceitful plots of the enemy to invade our children's lives through the destructive evil of Pokémon. His book Buying & Selling the Souls of Our Children *will enlighten you and call you into a deeper level of discernment needed to help call forth the prophetic destiny of this generation.*

Jim W. Goll
Founder, Ministry to the Nations, Antioch, Tennessee and Author, *The Lost Art of Intercession, Kneeling on the Promises*, and *Father Forgive Us!*

To my delight, John Paul Jackson has written a most insightful book about the game, Pokémon. For the sake of our children, I highly recommend that you read this book and heed this prophetic voice.

Daniel Kim
Pastor, River of Life Christian Fellowship
Pasadena, California

I am thrilled with John Paul Jackson's book, Buying & Selling the Souls of Our Children. *It's a must-read. It helps us understand just how spiritually destructive this "harmless" game really is. But more importantly, it teaches parents how to be media savvy and discerning.*

Holly McClure
Syndicated Film Critic, Southern California

John Paul Jackson has hit the nail on the head. The enemy of our souls is using this seemingly innocent game to seduce the next generation. Take this book and teach your children why Pokémon is nothing to be played with.

Steve Shultz
Founder, The Elijah List

Thank you, John Paul, for giving us a concise, comprehensive and well-documented tool. I encourage every parent, pastor and Christian to read this important book.

Eddie Smith
Founder and President, U.S. Prayer Track
Houston, Texas

Pokémon and other children's games would merit caution, investigation and, in most cases, abstinence merely on the basis of encouraging selfish, aggressive and violent behavior. John Paul Jackson has sounded a warning in this book that we all need to hear for ourselves, our children and their children. We need to heed the prophets among us—pointing us toward the God of heaven!

Jack Taylor
President, Dimensions Ministries, Melbourne, Florida

Buying & Selling the Souls of Our Children *exposes another thief wielding the counterfeit powers of Satan. With prophetic wisdom and insight, John Paul Jackson goes straight to the heart and uncovers the battle raging for the souls of our children.*

David Van Cronkhite
Founder, Blood-n-Fire International, Atlanta, Georgia

Also by John Paul Jackson

Needless Casualties of War

Buying & Selling the Souls of Our Children

John Paul Jackson

A Closer Look at Pokémon™

Published by Streams Publications, a division of Streams Ministries International, P.O. Box 101808, Ft. Worth, TX 76185, U.S.A. Tel: (817) 536-7799 Fax: (817) 536-7710 Web site: http://www.streamsministries.com

Published in the United Kingdom, its territories and the EC by Kingsway Publishing, a division of Kingsway Communications, Lottbridge Drove, Eastbourne, East Sussex BN23 6NT, England.

Library of Congress Catalog Card Number: 00-103847
ISBN 1-58483-015-8
Designed by Ed Tuttle
Printed on acid-free paper in the United States of America

For my beloved son, Micah,
and others of his prophetic generation

Come let us go up to the mountain of
the Lord, To the house of the God of
Jacob; He will teach us His ways, And
we shall walk in His paths.

Micah 4:2

Contents

Acknowledgements

This book would never have become a reality without the dedication, resourcefulness, encouragement and quiet resolve of my loving wife, Diane. Her skills, talents and wise counsel serve to undergird all that I do for the Kingdom of God.

I also wish to acknowledge Donna Higgins and her recently departed husband, Jerry, who invited me on their television show, Tentmakers. It was on their program that I first discussed the problems of Pokémon. I also want to thank Susan Martin, who along with the Higgins, provided creative inspiration that launched the beginning of this project.

I want to thank Amy Cook, who took my research and notes and helped to craft the manuscript; Brett Yates, who added his skills as the book developed editorially; Matt Boswell, who helped research and verify elements in the book; Ed Tuttle, whose striking and beautiful designs frame this book; and Carolyn Blunk, who provided editorial guidance in turning this manuscript into a book.

I also want to thank Margaret Jobe, Laurie Thompson, Sandra Mehmandost, Diane Schechner, Laura Smith, Dottie Hutcheson, Fenancia Tillema, Vicki Jackson, Shonda Jackson and Roxanne Stewart who contributed unselfishly of their time, talents and skills to type Pokémon descriptions or to painstakingly proofread the text in its final form.

And finally, I am deeply grateful to my partners in prayer and those who financially support this ministry. Thank you for linking arms with us, for such a time as this.

> Now thanks be to God who always leads us in triumph in Christ, and through us diffuses the fragrance of His knowledge in every place.
>
> *2 Corinthians 2:14*

Buying & Selling the Souls of Our Children

Awake,
you who sleep,
arise from the dead,
and **Christ** will
give you **light.**

Introduction

I began working on this book in response to being interviewed on a television program in Dallas, Texas concerning Pokémon, the immensely popular children's role-playing game, television show and feature film.

At the time, I was the father of an eleven-year-old son and I taught and ministered internationally—as I still do—on revelatory gifts and the supernatural. This book was my way of responding to questions about how to nurture prophetically gifted children and, in particular, about controversial games like Pokémon.

In recent years, our culture has developed an obsession with the dark side of the supernatural. Secular games, videos, television shows, movies and books often have "exchanged the truth of God for the lie" (Romans 1:25).

Fascination with the paranormal reflects a paradigm shift that has occurred in western civilization over the last few years. While it may seem as if we are living during a time of heightened spirituality, what is promoted in our culture is not Christianity. It's a form of New Age spirituality where pagan practices such as sorcery, necromancy, channeling, clairvoyance and psychic healing are being mainstreamed into society. Those who seek to proliferate these doctrines have chosen our children as their prime subjects.

Throughout Scripture, we are warned to "Give no regard to mediums and familiar spirits; do not seek after them, to be defiled by them: I am the Lord your God" (Leviticus 19:31). We are instructed to reject every form of spiritism as evil. However, many today consult psychics for major life decisions, such as whom to marry. Whenever we do that, we look to demons for advice and not to our loving heavenly Father.

Jesus predicted that a day would come when many would reject God's truth and accept Satan's counterfeit.

> For false christs and false prophets will rise and show signs and wonders to deceive, if possible, even the elect.
>
> *Mark 13:22*

The more I investigated and explored Pokémon, the more concerned and alarmed I became. I believe this game—and others like it—invites a demonic harasser to assault our children.

In our generation, God is raising up a prophetic ministry that was foretold in Scripture by the prophet Joel. He described a remarkable generation that would have the Spirit of God poured out on young and old alike (Joel 2:28-32). Under the anointing of the Holy Spirit, prophetic utterances would arise from even young children—not just those who are mature in the Lord. Although the Holy Spirit had rested upon prophets and priests, there had never been a massive outpouring of the Holy Spirit.

Our children and teenagers have an amazing destiny awaiting them. As they mature in Christ, they will walk in greater anointing and hear from God more clearly than previous generations. They will perform miraculous signs and wonders and accomplish great exploits for the Kingdom of God.

The enemy hates this. As a liar and deceiver, his goal is to steal, kill and destroy what is precious to God. To accomplish his goal, he often seeks out those who are most vulnerable. He never plays by the rules. He tries to deceive the curious through television, movies, videos and even the games children play.

Just as Satan devised a scheme to kill Moses, and later Jesus Christ, by influencing rulers to murder newborns (Exodus 1:16-22; Matthew 2:13-18), the devil seeks to silence future prophetic voices through abortion. He also tries to render them powerless through misuse of their gifts or to misdirect their gifts into his demonic arena.

Weaving a web of lies, Satan camouflages his deception and seductively indoctrinates the unsuspecting into the principles of his diabolical kingdom—one characterized by chaos, deceit, strife, rage, confusion, greed, and power.

What Satan cannot destroy, he seeks to defile and pervert for his own demonic use. If he can capture an individual's God-given gifts at an early age, then he can detour that person's potential destiny. Using appealing and seemingly harmless pursuits like Pokémon and other enchanting role-playing games to beguile children and to confuse or desensitize parents, our crafty foe sows his occultic seeds into their mental processes and heart attitudes.

My prayer in writing this book is that the Lord will use these insights to awaken a slumbering church about the end-time strategy of the enemy. I also seek to penetrate the increasing darkness of the hour with the light of Jesus Christ.

> We should no longer be children, tossed to and fro and carried about with every wind of doctrine, by the trickery of men, in the cunning craftiness of deceitful plotting...
>
> *Ephesians 4:14*

> And have no fellowship with the unfruitful works of darkness, but rather to expose them... All things that are exposed are made manifest by the light... Therefore He says: Awake, you who sleep, arise from the dead, and Christ will give you

Buying & Selling the Souls of Our Children

light. See then that you walk circumspectly, not as fools but as wise, redeeming the time, because the days are evil.

Ephesians 5:11-16

Our adversary
the devil walks
about like a
roaring lion,
seeking whom
he may devour

Chapter One

The War Over Souls

It is late Thursday afternoon. George, a fourth grader, and his friend Eric are lying on the floor, mesmerized by the scene before them. As they assume the role of magical creatures battling their way for control, they innocently invoke white magic and channel spirits to capture their opponents and become all-powerful. After all, it is *just* a game... Or is it?

While their parents regard this game as just a passing fad, an innocent pastime that religious fanatics like to attack, the two dark spirits hovering in a nearby corner know better. Undetected by the children, the larger of the two demons speaks.

"This is our children's discipleship program," he growls with a smirk of approval. "Through our enchanting games, these church kids are being taught all the wickedly wonderful vices of greed, vio-

1

lence, and rebellion. Just wait until they are older! They'll easily accept even darker powers! We simply have to convince their parents that we do not exist. What an ingenious plan our master has devised," he chuckles with sinister delight.

Down the street, several teenagers have graduated to more sophisticated role-playing games. Collecting Magic trading cards, they amuse themselves by spending time thinking deeply about dark, evil forces—how to control and use them.

Imaginative, inquisitive, and intelligent computer geeks, one of the boys decides to give the game a new twist. Drawing a pentagram in the dirt, he reads a Magic card while studying its detailed artwork. Speaking the name of a dark spirit, he asks it to enter them. Nearby, three spirits, who are waiting like hyenas to attack their prey, slide inside the boys' bodies and the unseen holocaust begins.

Deadly Enticement

Our children today are being lured into dabbling in the occult through role-playing games such as Pokémon, Digimon, Magic: The Gathering, and Dungeons & Dragons, as well as other fantasy and science fiction books, movies and television shows. While not all children who play these games will become servants of darkness, they are being taught New Age and neopaganism values. Many are being desensitized to the Holy Spirit and drawn like a magnet to the dark side of the supernatural.

The Great Deception

I am absolutely convinced that we are living during a time of great deception that is spoken of in Scripture (2 Thessalonians 2:3-12). Blindly following an ingenious counterfeit, many will stumble headlong into evil, unaware they are being deceived. Sadly, they will never stop to heed the warnings that foretell of the deception. Believing a lie, they will allow themselves to be hardened to the truth.

In centuries past, the apostle Paul foresaw a time arising over the Earth that would be marked by great deception. It would be a time that Satan would deceive even the elect, if that were possible (Matthew 24:24). Veiled by a magnificent illusion, Christians would have a difficult time recognizing the evil masquerade, were it not for the gifts of the Holy Spirit. As Paul lamented to the early church:

> But I fear, lest somehow, as the serpent deceived Eve by his craftiness, so your minds may be corrupted from the simplicity that is in Christ.
>
> *2 Corinthians 11:3*

One of Satan's names is "the serpent" (Matthew 23:33, Revelation 12:9). By way of that disguise, the devil enticed Eve into questioning God's warning. Over the years, his methods haven't changed much. He continues to lead mankind astray by clever arguments, vain imaginations and enticing allurements.

Soul Trading

The apostle John also described a time of great deception in the book of Revelation. In this startling vision, John watched as human beings were treated like cattle and the very souls of men were bought and sold (Revelation 18:13). By sorcery—power gained by the assistance of evil spirits—all the nations on Earth were tricked, defrauded and led astray.

> For your merchants were the great men of the
> Earth, for by your sorcery all the nations were
> deceived.
>
> *Revelation 18:23*

While sorcery conjures up images of adults practicing magic, witchcraft and occult rituals, children can be indoctrinated into sorcery at an early age. Ensnared in the bog of darkness, they will be unable to discern the darkness from the light, and thus be led astray from the truth. Having been spiritually anesthetized by a spirit of seduction, they will embrace what seems attractive and charming. In fact, seduction will *always* entice us to stray from a place of safety.

Scripture implores us to seek God and to cry out for wisdom and discernment (Proverbs 2:3). We are also commanded to train our children in the ways of God, so that when they are older they will not depart from that teaching. Even if our children do not

Buying & Selling the Souls of Our Children

understand everything that we teach, their spirits will absorb God's truth.

Don't be deceived. Our children's spirits will be receptive to evil principles and occult symbols woven into seemingly harmless games. It matters not if our children understand what the symbols mean. Demonic inroads will be made into their spirits.

By concealing his sorcery with cartoon characters, the enemy achieves his goals and deceives both parents and children. Scripture refers to this tactic as the wiles—trickery—of the devil (Ephesians 6:11).

Our Adversary

In *The Screwtape Letters*, C. S. Lewis warned of two great mistakes that humans often make in dealing with the devil. One is to have an unhealthy fascination with him. The other is to be completely ignorant of his existence and his schemes.[1]

Throughout Scripture, we are exhorted not to be ignorant of the devil's schemes (2 Corinthians 2:11). Rather, we are to remain clear-minded and attentive because our "adversary the devil walks about like a roaring lion, seeking whom he may devour" (1 Peter 5:8). We are also instructed to be wise as snakes to evil's seductive ploys, but innocent as doves to sin's pleasures (Matthew 10:16). Scripture encourages us to expose the works of darkness and to walk wisely as children of light (Ephesians 5:11,13).

The Beginning of Wisdom

True intimacy with God will bring wisdom and discernment. Jesus did nothing of his own initiative, but He only did what He saw the Father was doing (John 5:19-20). The works of Jesus were born out of intimacy with the Father. Likewise, as we abide in the Father and He in us, God's ways will be revealed to us.

As the Holy Spirit dwells within us, we will be led into a deeper relationship with God. We will know Him as our Father. His Word will be internalized in our mind and written on our hearts. Our actions will reflect our knowledge of God's ways (Jeremiah 31:33-34). He will impart a spirit of wisdom and revelation (Ephesians 1:17). As a result, the light inside us will shine forth even in the midst of great darkness.

As it was in the beginning, conflict between the Kingdom of God and the kingdom of Satan rages over the souls of mankind. In the days ahead, it will intensify. Darkness will blanket the Earth, and deep darkness will cover the people (Isaiah 60:2).

Test all things;
hold fast what
is good.
Abstain from
every form
of evil.

Chapter Two

What's All the Fuss About Pokémon?

A few years ago, hardly anyone in the United States had heard of Pokémon. Today, it's all the rage among kids, age twelve and under. Imported from Japan, Pokémon—short for Pocket Monsters—is a sophisticated game that centers around staging battles with various Pokémon. The goal of players is to become the "number one Pokémon Master in the world."[2]

Each Pokémon has different magical powers and fighting abilities. They range in size from one foot to twenty-eight feet tall and can weigh as little as a feather or as much as 1,914 pounds. Each creature is endowed with the ability to inflict harm on its opponent. Even a tiny creature can launch a ferocious and brutal attack. Each can also evolve into a creature with more menacing powers.

2 Read "Pocket Monsters" every time Pokémon occurs

At the simplest level, Pokémon is about acquiring power. An assumption in the game is the more Pokémon you have, the greater power you possess. Children accumulate such power by dueling with other players and racking up points. In the trading card game, children are encouraged to carry their Pokémon cards with them and to use the power listed on the cards.[3] A similar belief is held by those who carry magical charms or fetishes for empowerment.

Kabutops – Pokémon No. 141

This character slashes prey with its claws and drains body fluids. Many children often identify with imaginary characters. Is this what we want our children to identify with?

Fueling the Frenzy

In the trading card game, each card depicts a colorful cartoon creature with special powers. Players collect these creatures and send them into battle against their opponent's creatures. While some cards are commonly found, others are rare and can cost hundreds of dollars—which serves to fuel the card-collecting frenzy. The quest for more Pokémon will only grow, as Nintendo of America releases a gold and silver product line this year that promises dozens more species of Pokémon.

Some kids are stabbing, beating, and stealing in an addictive drive to collect the coveted cards. A nine-year-old stabbed a thirteen-year-old in a clash over cards in New York. A fourteen-year-old Canadian boy suffered a similar knife wound to the shoulder. While in Florida, a seventh-grade student was expelled for attacking a teacher who took away his cards.[4]

One teacher from Connecticut shared with me about a fifth grade student who attacked another student with a razor blade. When she talked with him, he claimed to be inspired by various Pokémon that attack their opponents by slashing them with a razor-sharp instrument. He also said that he was seeking power over his classmates.

A Quest for Power

In their quest to accumulate cards, players seek to increase their power base and rack up "hit points (HP)" denoted on each card. These hit points depict the degree of damage that a particular Pokémon character can inflict.

Four different kinds of trading cards exist in the game. Basic Pokémon cards are played directly from a player's hand. They activate a specific Pokémon character. Evolution cards are used to make a Pokémon evolve to a higher or more powerful level. Energy cards empower a Pokémon to carry out an attack. Trainer cards are used once to accomplish something, and then discarded.

Colored Energy

To launch an attack, a player must have the required energy. Energy is classified into different types with a corresponding color—grass energy (green), fire energy (red), water energy (blue), lightning energy (yellow), psychic energy (purple), fighting energy (brown) and colorless energy (clear).

Mounting an Attack

As players pit their Pokémon against one another, they are encouraged to use rage, poison, fire, etc. Furthermore, they can attack by sending a curse of amnesia, confusion, paralysis or sleep. Even species classified outside the psychic category can attack with psychic powers such as hypnosis, mind reading, teleporting, and inflicting headaches on others.

These creatures mimic the kind of warfare practiced in the occult—chanting, using mantras and inflicting curses upon people. Thereby, the methods of staging battles that were once considered as evil by our culture—as well as by the Word of God—are used by Pokémon players as if they were good.

Hypno, Pokémon No. 097

When it locks eyes with the opponent, it will use a mix of psychic moves such as hypnosis and confusion. This creature uses occult, psychic powers to attack its victims. Do we want our children to be flirting with such powers, even in role-playing?

Pokégods

When using the Game Shark and computer video game, Pokémon can evolve to achieve god-like power over others. When playing on a Game Shark, players enter different codes listed on various internet websites to enable their Pokémon to evolve into Pokégods.

Even Ash, the ten-year-old hero of the game, can become a god. In talking with many children who play Pokémon, the character they most want to become is Ash. As they role-play—acting out the thoughts and feelings of the character—they gradually begin to embrace the thought that they, too, can become a god, as they evolve to a higher life form and take on higher powers by conquering others.

The Counterfeit Trinity

Ash, for example, can evolve into Dodrio, a creature that resembles

Dodrio, Pokémon No. 085

A three-headed creature that attacks victims by pecking them with rage. While two heads sleep, one is awake. By overcoming other Pokémon with violence, Dodrio has the potential to become a god. What is this teaching our children?

a bird with three heads. Interestingly, Dodrio's height and weight are the dimensions of an average-sized man. Dodrio is the only Pocket Monster with three heads—an interesting allusion to a counterfeit Trinity.

In the Holy Trinity, the Holy Spirit is sent to indwell, empower, defend, teach and lead followers of Jesus Christ. The same may be said about the counterfeit trinity, except that the empowerment is dark in its nature.

Subtly, Pokémon promotes the belief that man can become like God—a philosophy that is also promoted in Buddhism and New Age religions. It was also the enticement that Satan offered to Adam and Eve in the Garden of Eden. It was this temptation that inspired the people of Babylon to construct the Tower of Babel. It's a ploy that Satan has used on many unsuspecting souls. Will our children be the next target of his evil deception?

Soul Projection

Another ominous trait of Dodrio is that it's the only creature in which players are enabled to project their soul. Therefore, a child who plays the game through Ash, can project his soul into Dodrio and become a Pokégod.

This practice of projecting one's soul is found in many eastern religions. It's also a common practice in witchcraft. This practice is one of many troubling elements found in Pokémon. It programs our children to accept occultic practices such as astro-projection and soul exchanges taught in pagan spiritual rites.

Whenever role-playing games encourage children to act out the thoughts and feelings of a character, their spirit plays an active part in the game. What if a child decided to use soul projection as an active part of his or her playtime? Would it suggest to a child that such occult practices were valuable? Would a child become confused about godly ways, and thus, perceive evil as "good" and good as "evil"?

To further understand the latent dangers of Pokémon, let's examine the philosophies behind the game.

There shall not
be found among you
anyone who...
practices witchcraft,
or a soothsayer,
or one who
interprets omens,
or a sorcerer,
or one who
conjures spells...

Chapter Three

Philosophies Behind Pokémon

It was only a stone idol bought on a vacation while in India. The people who bought it weren't Hindu. To them, it was merely exotic art. However, after placing the statue in their home, strange things began to happen. They began having disturbing dreams. Their beloved cat mysteriously died. A feeling of depression and fear permeated the house. It wasn't long before they both became ill.

When a discerning friend identified the source of trouble—the Indian artifact—the couple quickly disposed of it and repented for bringing it into their home. Finally, they were delivered from the demonic attack that wreaked havoc in their lives.

While the couple did not worship the stone artifact, dark spirits and a dark philosophy were attached to it. Furthermore, the stone idol opened doors for the demonic realm to harass them. In a similar way, demonic attacks come from a door we open, knowingly or unknowingly. Simply bringing a pagan object into your home can have sinister results.

While many Christians would not allow their children to bring a pentagram or voodoo doll into their homes, they have unknowingly opened a door to the demonic. They have done this simply by allowing their children to play with games that are pagan, and that employ principles practiced in occult worship. It's my belief that Pokémon, and games that bear resemblance to it, open demonic doors that can unleash spiritual attacks on the unsuspecting, as well as on those who embrace the dark side.

Demonic Invasion of Dreams

One door that is opened to the demonic realm through Pokémon occurs in the realm of dreams. In Pokémon, for example, an evolved ghost named Haunter can hypnotize and drain the energy from its victim. Then, the creature eats the dreams of its opponent. This concept of stealing dreams can be found in several eastern religions. It is often referred to as an "energy vampire," which may also explain why Haunter has vampire-like fangs.

One of the scariest issues for individuals who have renounced various forms of witchcraft is how the enemy can enter into their dreams to attack them. It's a ploy of the enemy. Yet, our children are being encouraged to accept and practice this strategy in this seemingly innocent game of Pokémon.

Haunter, Pokémon No. 093

Through psychic powers, this ghost can create confusion and place a curse of sleep on its enemies. It also has the ability to eat dreams. Do demonic spirits consider it just a game when they are invoked? Is it any accident that many children playing Pokémon have had recurring nightmares?

Night Terrors

The consequences of such role-playing strategies on our children are profound. Several parents have shared with me that, in the initial stages of the game, it was common for their children to have nightmares and wake up screaming in fear.

After briefly speaking on this subject at a conference, a mother came up to me the following day. With great excitement she said, "Last night my son's nightmares instantly stopped!" She had previously removed all Pokémon paraphernalia from her son's room, but his night terrors still remained. As she prayed, the Lord gave her a supernatural word of knowledge:

her son had hidden a Pokémon card among his stack of base-ball cards. After attending my conference, she returned home and spoke with her son about the game. He reluctantly confessed to keeping a card. After explaining the spiritual problems associated with the game, they went to their fireplace together and burned the remaining card. For the first time in months, her son slept through the night peacefully. When he awoke, he was in a good mood, which had not been true since the nightmares began.

Psychic Dangers

Potential psychic dangers exist for children who play this game. Consider the Pokémon creature called, Psyduck, who is described on the Pokédex—an encyclopedia of information about each Pokémon—as mesmerizing his opponents with a piercing stare and unleashing a barrage of pent-up mental energy.[5] By sitting for hours in front of a computer screen playing Pokémon, our children resemble sitting ducks as Satan launches his attack, like Psyduck. He mesmerizes them with color animations and barrages their minds with psychic energy.

While this may seem like an innocent game, an evil spirit is the driving force behind the game. The enemy doesn't care if someone innocently opens such spiritually dark doors; he only cares that the doors to our souls are open.

The Cross Is Seen as Powerless

Let's examine how Pokémon regards the primary symbol and principle in Christianity—that of the cross. In a disturbing, yet revealing, television episode of Pokémon, several kids try to defeat a fanged ghost Pokémon. While holding up a shining gold cross, along with some garlic and a wooden stake, the ghost merely laughs. But as the sun—one of the gods worshipped in Japan—begins to rise over the horizon, the fanged monster's power is defeated.

For Christians, the cross symbolizes victory. It's where Satan and his power were defeated. However, in the world of Pokémon, the cross symbolizes weakness and defeat. It is shown as having absolutely no power over the Pokémon. In fact, it depicts the creature as having power over the cross.

This philosophy is slowly and subtly being instilled in our children. It's a clever strategy of the enemy. As his onslaught continues, our children may simply dismiss the cross as a powerless relic and look to creation and other gods for empowerment.

Rooted in Shinto Buddhism

Pokémon is rooted in Japanese culture and religious beliefs. Shinto, as a belief system, was incorporated into Japanese Buddhist practices beginning in the sixth century. Shinto is primarily a form of nature worship, where creative elements, such as earth, sun, water, rocks and trees are worshipped and personified. They believe these elements have a god behind their power. Interestingly, these features are also central elements portrayed in the game of Pokémon.

Summoning Evil Spirits

In Shinto, kami (spirits) are summoned through chanting and music. Chanting is a form of self-hypnosis and opens a demonic doorway to a person's soul. In Pokémon, players are encouraged to chant the names of their Pocket Monsters. Some Pokémon also chant or sing songs as a means to hypnotize or lull their victim to sleep.

In Shinto, it is believed that kami help fight off evil spirits. Japanese festivals honor these spirits. It is believed that by appeasing them, people will be kept from harm. However, after taking hundreds of people through deliverance, I have noticed that protection from evil spirits *only* comes through the name of Jesus. It does not come by honoring or appeasing evil spirits. Whenever an evil spirit removes another, it's a matter of a spirit being outranked. Thereby, a weaker demon is traded for a more powerful demon.

Evolution and Reincarnation

Hindu and Buddhist concepts of evolution and reincarnation are also found in Pokémon. As with other occultic religions, Buddhism teaches that we are constantly being reincarnated into higher forms of life. Therefore, mankind does not need a savior because we are divinely evolving to become more god-like.

Playing Pokémon also reinforces the false theory of evolution that is taught in our public schools. Subtly, children who role-play this game are encouraged by the thought that everything evolves. Such thinking also leads our children into accepting the false philosophy that we have had previous lives. However, the philosophy of reincarnation contradicts the truth of God:

> It is appointed for men to die once, but after this the judgment.

> *Hebrews 9:27*

Use of Sorcery

Even more disturbing is how the game of Pokémon employs sorcery. Pagan religions believe we receive strength from the five elements of earth, fire, water, air, and spirit. Each element forms the five points of the pentagram, with spirit serving as the star's top point.

In sorcery, these elements are manipulated by magic. In the game of Pokémon, these elements are manipulated by the use of "energy cards," which empower the creatures. As Christians, our children need to be taught that those who belong to Jesus draw their power from God, not creation. We trust in God's power to protect us, not the power of the elements, channeled through spirits.

Enslaving Demons

In New Age paganism and the occult, it is commonly believed that spirit guides, messengers, and elementals (or spirits) can be summoned to do things for a trainer or practitioner. Spirit guides watch and tell a trainer what it sees. These spirits guard the trainer, fight-off other spirits or elementals, and carry out assignments given by the trainer.

Dangerous parallels exist between the world of Pokémon and that of the occult. A pagan trainer can capture free elementals—much like Pokémon trainers capture Pocket Monsters—and build relationships with them for future use. This same relationship is also found in Wicca or Witchcraft.

Wiccan Circles

In Wicca, guardians, known as Watchtowers, are summoned into a protective circle until called upon to fight off "bad" spirits. In Pokémon, the creatures are held in a Pokéball until the trainer summons them to fight.

In mature forms of witchcraft, one advances to higher levels by conquering demons in other people to make them their slaves. The master practitioner can then project thoughts into the slave as his demons communicate orders to the slave demons in the other person. This principle is being taught to our children in the way

Pokémon capture other Pokémon. It falls under the deeper things of Satan we are warned about in Revelation 2.

Witches and shamans, who claim to project themselves into animals, recommend that only master practitioners do these things because an individual is not the master of the spirits, just as trainers are not masters of the Pocket Monsters. They warn that such spirits, once summoned, can be hard to get rid of, and may require an exorcism to be freed of an "evil one".

Tree of the Knowledge of Good and Evil

Some parents are saying, "Pokémon is just about the battle between good and evil." But if "good" monsters are using psychic, occultic, and sadistic methods to win over "evil" monsters, how do you separate good from evil? Isn't it all from the same tree—the Knowledge of Good and Evil? What does this teach the child?

If we think that only overt evil is sinful, then we fail to realize that not everything perceived as "good" is from God and is spiritually beneficial. Something perceived as "good" can actually be detrimental. Remember, the enemy used the "Tree of the Knowledge of Good and Evil" to entice Adam and Eve. He still uses it today. All too often, we think that if it is "good" then it must be God or from God. However, there is a way that seems right or good to us, but its end is the way of death (Proverbs 14:12; 16:25).

The Evil of Sorcery

What I have described previously are occultic practices. Tactics such as inflicting pain through slashing, psychic power, fits of rage, and "draining the life force" out of an opponent belong to Satan, not to God. As Christians, we should teach our children to bring life to others, not drain it from them.

When Jesus cast the demons out of a blind and mute person, the Pharisees said, "It is only by Beelzebub, the prince of demons, that this fellow drives out demons" (Matthew 12:24). Jesus replied, "If Satan drives out Satan, he is divided against himself."

So why should we allow our children to even pretend such methods work—driving out evil spirits by the use of other evil spirits? Whose purpose does this serve: God's or Satan's?

Idolatry

Most Christians realize that Buddhism and other pagan religions are forms of religious idolatry. The Bible is full of examples of this type of sin, and of God's judgment upon those who practice it. Therefore, we won't take time to build a case against the sin of idolatry. This issue should be self-evident to Christians.

Modern Witchcraft

It is surprising how many Christians are deceived concerning the dangers of witchcraft. In the last ten years, witchcraft has had a surge of popularity in our culture. Just take a look at the astronomical sales of the Harry Potter children's books, where the hero and his friends cast spells, read crystal balls and turn themselves into animals.

Also disturbing is the popularity of television shows like *Charmed*, *Buffy the Vampire Slayer* or *Sabrina, the Teenage Witch* and movies like *The Craft* that blatantly promote a modernized witchcraft. Their heroines are young, hip and alluring witches. They serve as role models and train our children how to practice sorcery. It may surprise you to learn that in schools across our nation, clubs for witches outnumber Christian clubs. The blatantly defiant attitude of those practitioners is growing more hostile every day.

So, let's take a moment to examine how seriously God views this sin.

> There shall not be found among you anyone who makes his son or his daughter pass through the fire, or one who practices witchcraft, or a soothsayer, or one who interprets omens, or a sorcerer, or one who conjures spells, or a medium, or a spiritist, or one who calls up the dead. For all who do these things are an abomination

to the Lord, and because of these abominations
the Lord your God drives them out before you.

Deuteronomy 18:10-12

God does not consider sorcery and witchcraft to be innocent fun for adults, let alone for children. He confronts it in the strongest of terms and requires us to do the same.

Creator of Pokémon

To further understand Pokémon, it might be helpful to mention a few things about its creator, Satoshi Tajiri. He is described as a misfit, and is the sort of person who isolates from the rest of society—prefering to live in a virtual world of video games or comic books.[6] As such individuals detach from personal relationships, they often accumulate things to fill the void. The more they accumulate, the better they feel about themselves. This underlying philosophy is woven into the game of Pokémon.

Accumulation and Power

Accumulation and power fuels the popularity of this game. A child knows that the more Pokémon he can conquer, the more power he has and the greater his level of achievement. The attributes of greed are cleverly embedded in the game's principles.

It also assures the game's owners and distributors of many repeat sales in the future. Pokémon's registered trademark slogan is "Gotta catch 'em all," which translates into, "Gotta buy 'em all." Pokémon truly reinforces the materialistic mantra of our culture— the more you have, the better your life will be.

Ensnared into Buying Pokémon

One night while talking about Pokémon on a Christian television program, a man called the broadcast, outraged that I was speaking against the game. He had just spent $800 on Pokémon toys, trading cards and video games for his grandchildren for Christmas presents. For several months, he had spent $100 each month on Pokémon gift items. Since he had invested his money in the game, he asked, "How can Pokémon be so wrong when I have spent so much money?" The man was trapped and he didn't even know it.

Spirits of Greed and Strife

The spirits of greed and strife seem to inspire the game's philosophy. Jesus did not consider greed a trivial sin. He soberly warned His followers:

> Take heed and beware of covetousness, for one's

life does not consist in the abundance of the things he possesses.

Luke 12:15

For this you know, that no fornicator, unclean person, nor covetous man who is an idolater, has any inheritance in the kingdom of Christ and God.

Ephesians 5:5

Covetousness—an extreme desire to acquire or possess—as well as greed are prevalent attitudes exhibited by children playing Pokémon. By planting in children's minds they must "catch 'em all," the worldly values of greed and covetousness are encouraged and promoted throughout the game.

Since covetousness often leads to strife, it's not surprising that fighting is the primary activity in the game.

As parents, we need to exercise our God-given authority as overseers of our children and take time to seriously consider the philosophy behind all games. We also need to examine the content of role-playing games and determine if such role-playing adversely affects the spiritual growth and development of our children.

Woe to those
who call evil good
and good evil,
who put darkness
for light and
light for darkness.

Chapter Four

The Seduction of Role Playing

I n remote Arctic villages, the native Inuits have a way of baiting and killing wolves. Taking a hunting knife, they cover it with blood. When the blood freezes, the knife is covered with another layer of blood and the process is repeated. After the knife is covered with many layers of frozen blood, the handle is placed in the snow with the point of the blade facing upward.

Drawn by the smell of blood, a wolf finds the knife and begins to lick the blade. The animal is so consumed by its craving for blood that it keeps licking until it begins to lacerate its tongue on the sharp edge of the knife's blade. The wolf, however, obsessed with the taste of blood, does not realize that the blood it is consuming is its own. The wolf eventually dies, bleeding to death, not realizing that the instrument of its death was its own lust.

Like the wolf licking the blood-covered knife, children can unwittingly find themselves in a dangerous place as they become a channel for demonic activity.

Fantasy or Reality

Occult-oriented role-playing, fantasy and simulation games such as Pokémon, Digimon, Magic: The Gathering, and Dungeons & Dragons are dominating the market today. It's a multi-billion dollar industry.

These games foster a sense of personal power and authority through identification with godlike superheroes. Often the line between fantasy and reality becomes blurred. Much like the wolf, the deeper you get sucked in, the greater the potential for more lacerating consequences.

Many have documented how the Dungeons & Dragons role-playing game has led to deeper involvement in the occult. Sean Sellers, at twelve years old, delved into the dark fantasy world of Dungeons & Dragons and actively studied Satanism. After dedicating his life to Satan, Sean executed his mother, stepfather and a convenience store clerk when he was only sixteen. Convicted on three counts of murder, he became the youngest inmate on Oklahoma's death row. While in prison, Sean became a Christian and began speaking out about the dangers of Dungeons & Dragons.

In such role-playing games, the child wields the power and

becomes the master. From that perspective, it's a simple jump to embrace similar principles found in witchcraft and Satanism.

Psychological Aspects of the Game

Psychologists are aware of the potential dangers of role-playing. Such imagination and make-believe can cause children to emotionally experience—or simulate—the role being played. The rules and rewards learned in the game can influence a child's development of new habits and repetitive responses. Day after day, this powerful psychological process of reinforcement manipulates a child's thoughts, feelings, and actions until his or her personality changes. A new way of thinking that emerges seems almost natural. Strongholds begin to be solidified in a child's mind.

In his book, *Healing the Nations*, John Sandford defines a stronghold as a practiced way of thinking that has become ingrained and automatic. It has a life of its own. Regarding such strongholds, he writes:

> Strongholds create tunnel vision. It is as though the person is wearing blinders so he cannot see anything outside his limited perspective. Strongholds twist the words of the Bible to make inapplicable or irrelevant any

> glimmers of truth. The person might say, "Yes
> I know, but that doesn't apply to me," or, "I
> don't think it means that"—when the truth of
> God's Word is as obvious as the nose on his face.
> Strongholds send out smoke screens. They cause
> a person to obscure and confuse the subject at
> hand. They make straight lines crooked and
> clear ideas murky.[7]

If Pokémon cultivates greedy, combative, and obsessive tendencies in our children, Christian parents should be concerned. The Bible says we are known by our fruit, which comes as an outgrowth of activity. Those who practice anger, hatred, envy, selfish ambition, sorcery and dissensions are not operating in the fruits of the Holy Spirit (Galatians 5:19-23).

Other repercussions from the game occur when children are encouraged through role-playing to kill, poison, attack with rage, and destroy to the point they sear their conscience and dull their moral and spiritual sensitivity.

Further psychological consequences can come from inundating oneself in role-playing games that promote violence and occultic beliefs and practices. Thomas Redecki, a psychiatrist and chairman of the National Coalition on Television Violence, has given expert testimony at several murder trials on the effect that some role-playing games had on those playing them:

> I've found multiple instances of attitudes, values and perceptions of reality that were strongly influenced by immersion in these games. When someone spends 15 to 30 hours-per-week dreaming of how to go out and kill your opponents and steal treasure, it's not surprising that the desire to act out in real life occurs.[8]

Role-playing games can desensitize children toward violence. Distinctions between good and evil become blurred. What was once unthinkable behavior becomes acceptable or even normal. This is known as Gradualism. It suggests that eventually children will condone certain behaviors that were once prohibited. Thus, they will conclude that "the end justifies the means."

The Frog in the Pot

Remember the parable of the frog that jumped into a cooking pot on the stove? At first, the water was temperate, even comfortable for the frog who was stranded in this strange human abode. Gradually, the temperature became warmer and more uncomfortable. When the water began to boil, the frog didn't notice. It never felt the increasing heat. Despite the fact its skin was burning, the frog wasn't alarmed. Not long thereafter, the frog lost consciousness and became dinner that night. In a similar way, what is true in the physical sense is true in the spiritual or ethical sense. In a culture of increasing darkness and depravity, it's easy to drift along, unaware of impending danger, until it's too late.

Beyond Pokémon

Some educators and parents have noticed that the frenzy of Pokémon is fueling a craving for other role-playing games such as Magic: The Gathering, considered the most popular game of the decade. With an estimated fan base of more than six million, Magic players around the globe vie for college scholarships and cash prizes in tournaments held in exciting locations such as Hawaii, Kuala Lampur and Disney's Wide World of Sports in Orlando, Florida. However, this game teaches children how to conjure demons, cast spells, disable and kill their opponents and fantasize about brutal, dark forces.

According to one report, a mother shared that her son's elementary school was using Magic to teach math. Although she refused to allow her son to play Magic, another student gave him a trading card called, "Soul Exchange". Artwork on the card depicted a spirit rising from a grave and the morbid instruction on the card told players to "sacrifice a white creature." Her son also said that on the playground, children would "summon" the forces on the cards by raising sticks into the air and saying, "Spirits, enter me." They called it "being possessed," and thought it was great fun.[9]

An eleven-year-old gave up playing the video game after realizing the mesmerizing effect that Magic had on her as she battled entities using witchcraft and channeling.[10]

Flirting with Evil

Channeling spirits has been something that has existed for thousands of years. Meddling in the spirit realm is very dangerous and even fantasizing about it can be precarious. Inviting "familiar spirits" is an activity of mediums and sorcerers. If you don't believe your child is channeling spirits when he is playing Pokémon, then you are being deceived. Channeling is part of the role-playing aspect of the game.

Is there such a thing as innocent role playing or dabbling with things of the occult? John and Mark Sandford, counselors who have worked for many years in the area of deliverance, think not. In their best-selling book, *A Comprehensive Guide to Deliverance and Inner Healing*, they write:

> To enter anything occult is always and immediately to step into the demonic. Demons take occult involvement not only as an automatic invitation to inhabit but as a legal contract to do so. There is no safe dabbling, no harmless experimentation, however it may be masked, even as "scientific inquiry."[11]

Dabbling with the occult is like playing with fire. Even if your intentions are innocent, you'll be burned. Merely scratching the surface of the occult is like opening Pandora's box.

Consequences of such occult tinkering include insomnia, sleep disturbances, nightmares, annoying inner voices, reoccurring accidents, physical illnesses, memory lapses, family turmoils, financial problems, and generational curses.[12]

God has strong warnings about such dabbling. The Old Testament forbids any involvement in the occult—with divination, witchcraft, charms, familiar spirits, wizards, necromancy, psychics—because it is an abomination to the Lord (Deuteronomy 18:10-12).

In the New Testament, when the apostle Paul confronted a wizard, he called him a son of the devil:

> O full of all deceit and all fraud, you son of the devil, you enemy of all righteousness, will you not cease perverting the straight ways of the Lord?
>
> *Acts 13:10*

The apostle Paul wasn't just name-calling. He was revealing the spirit that operated through the wizard. These same deceptive spirits are at work today, trying to lead children down a crooked path, instead of the straight path God has marked for them to follow.

Evolution, reincarnation, sorcery and psychic power, which are blatantly promoted in Pokémon, are among Satan's deceptions.

Scripture warns us to have nothing to do with these counterfeit acts of darkness.

> Woe to those who call evil good and good evil, who put darkness for light and light for darkness, who put bitter for sweet and sweet for bitter.

Isaiah 5:20

Beware lest anyone cheat you through philosophy and empty deceit, according to the tradition of men, according to the basic principles of the world, and not according to Christ.

Chapter Five

Obsessed with the Game

In a television episode of *Star Trek: The Next Generation* called, "The Game," a female alien introduces an addictive video game to one of the crew members of the USS Enterprise. Soon, everyone is seduced by the game. By wearing visors, they play the game using their minds. This game stimulates their brains so that they become physically addicted to it. Crew members become obsessed with reaching higher levels in the game. Advancing to these levels consumes every conversation on the ship and soon becomes the sole means of relating to one another.

As everyone becomes ensnared by the game, the alien is able to manipulate them and take over the ship. Salvation comes when a boy on the ship discovers what is really happening and exposes the enemy's counterfeit scheme.

In a similar way, Satan seeks to infiltrate and dominate our minds and our homes by what may appear to be innocent amusement. The game is so beguiling, it becomes an obsession. If you don't believe me, try taking Pokémon away from your children and see how they respond. Is such addiction born of the Spirit of God or of the devil?

Can a child repeatedly act out behavior which God has declared evil without numbing his or her own conscience? Consider the following story and what happened to the people involved.

Enchanting Ploys

Once upon a time in a far-away oriental kingdom, there was a witch who wanted to place a curse upon those living in the land. She knew that if she overtly cursed the kingdom, she would likely get burned at the stake. So, she decided to be coy and subtle about her scheme. The witch knew the people in the walled capital city loved the theatre, so she organized a puppet show. However, this puppet show was enchanted.

Each day, people were drawn to the puppet show and were mesmerized. News of the puppet show reached the king, and so the witch was invited to perform in the palace. Eventually strange things began to happen within the kingdom. As the puppets acted out violent skits, the people within the kingdom found themselves imitating the puppets. Soon, the kingdom was torn apart by violence and strife. Thus, the witch covertly divided a kingdom by appealing to what had become the people's passion.

Gyarados, Pokémon No. 130

Uses rage as its weapon. A child playing with this creature learns to gain victory and power over others by employing rage. Is this what we want our children learning? Is this what we want our children using in real life?

Invoking the Spirit of Rage

Like the tale I have just shared, two main themes in Pokémon are violence and strife. One Pokémon, Gyarados, is a huge and vicious dragon-like creature. He is described as being "capable of destroying entire cities in a rage." In Scripture, dragons always represent Satan and evil. Furthermore, Satan is described in Scripture as a raging enemy who destroys and devours (1 Peter 5:8; Revelation 12:9).

A child playing Pokémon may be enticed to use rage like Gyarados, to get what he or she wants. Children occasionally use rage on their parents to get what they want. But as parents, we should not encourage such behavior.

> He who is slow to anger is better than the mighty, and he who rules his spirit than he who takes a city.

Proverbs 16:32

Furthermore, the apostle Paul writes that "outbursts of wrath" are defined as a work of the flesh, along with idolatry, sorcery, hatred, dissensions, and selfish ambition (Galatians 5:20). All of these evil virtues are promoted in Pokémon.

Among the 151 species of Pokémon, thirty-one gain control by rage or fury and twenty-one gain control by slashing or stabbing. Although twelve Pokémon are classified as "psychic," sixty-five species use psychic energy to dominate others.

The apostle Paul continues in Galatians 5 to warn that those who practice such things will not inherit the Kingdom of God. Practice is defined by the dictionary as repeated performance of an activity in order to learn or perfect a skill. When Pokémon becomes a daily ritual for a child, the values and philosophy of the game are being practiced. What is the result of such practice? A child could lose his or her sensitivity to the Holy Spirit's conviction and fall prey more easily to deception.

Consider this warning to our generation:

> Now the Spirit expressly says that in latter times some will depart from the faith, giving heed to deceiving spirits and doctrines of demons.
>
> *1 Timothy 4:1*

How would a Christian fall away from the faith and be seduced by deceiving spirits and the doctrines of demons? Would it happen all at once or gradually? Do you think that we could be living in such a time as this?

Discipled in Pokémon

Instead of training to be Pokémon masters, our children should be trained to follow the Master—Jesus Christ. A teacher at a Christian school noticed that many students could recite the 151 Pokémon characters and list their attributes; yet, these same students had difficulty memorizing a single verse of Scripture, or even multiplication tables.

The Power of Meditation

Memorization is the first step in the process of meditation. Whatever ideas and beliefs upon which we ponder and reflect often become internalized in our behavior.

Why do you suppose that marketing gurus of various role-playing games encourage children to memorize the names and capabilities of their characters? Could it be to create a sense of community around the game and to make new disciples?

Unfortunately, the views being espoused by the secular entertainment industry are training our children in the fruits of darkness. Why do you think the Bible encourages us to not forget, to hide away, to retain, to inscribe on our hearts, to meditate on the Word of God? Perhaps because memorization shapes our attitudes and actions.

One way or the other, our children are going to be trained. It's up to us to assure they are trained in godliness and to resist gratifying their sinful nature and its fleshly impulses.

How can children cultivate the peace of God in their heart, if their playtime activity encourages rage, fury, strife, and confusion? How can they experience fullness of joy, if their activities grieve the Holy Spirit because they show no reverence for what pleases Him? What fruit should we be cultivating in the lives of our children?

Scripture provides a list of the spiritual fruit of the Holy Spirit:

> But the fruit of the Spirit is love, joy, peace, longsuffering, kindness, goodness, faithfulness, gentleness, self-control. Against such there is no law. And those who are Christ's have crucified the flesh (sinful nature) with its passions and desires.
>
> *Galatians 5:22*

Killing All Fleshly Desires

As Christians, we are called to die to fleshly passions and desires, not merely to actual deeds. Sensual passions and desires are the seeds that produce evil behavior.

Did you realize that whatever we fantasize about matters to God? He is intimately aware and involved in our spiritual development. As Christians, it is critical that we censor our imaginations, because wrong thoughts can easily become wrong attitudes that give birth to sinful actions. Emotions can manifest with equal force, whether incited by fantasy or reality. This fact alone fuels the pornography industry. Whatever we gaze upon with our eyes, feeds our imagination. One writer in Scripture prayed and asked God, "Turn away my eyes from looking at worthless things, and revive me in Your way" (Psalm 119:37).

Cultural Bombardment

Many Christians have been seduced by a massive global entertainment industry that seems to parallel Babylon. Living in a post-modern world, morality arises from a particular situation and is often defined by "group think"—a consensus of the majority opinion. This world is a far cry from a biblical worldview, where life is to be lived within God's moral limits.

Because it seems morally clean, some Christians may justify

their children playing Pokémon or watching its cartoons. On first appearances, it doesn't involve anything R-rated—sex, profanity or gory violence. However, what feels right by the world's standards is not always right in God's eyes. In fact, the apostle Paul cautions us:

> Beware lest anyone cheat you through philosophy and empty deceit, according to the tradition of men, according to the basic principles of the world, and not according to Christ.
>
> *Colossians 2:8*

Daily, our culture bombards our children with entertainment that reflects worldly philosophies and values. A Christian's resolve to live a holy life is often weakened by the battering ram of cultural compromise. They are seduced into drifting away from that which is holy and good.

Gratifying the Flesh

As author Berit Kjos has written, "It's hard to teach restraint to children who are begging for gratification. Wanting to please rather than overreact, we flinch at the thought of being called censors once again."[13]

Unfortunately, some parents would rather give their approval to role-playing games such as Pokémon than risk being labeled "intolerant". Feeling pressured by society, they would rather their children be seen as "cool" than "uncool". However, as Christians, we are not called to blend in with our culture but to stand out as a counter-culture. We are to be salt and light to the world. As parents, we must evaluate what comes into our homes according to the unchanging yardstick of Scripture, not according to the slippery slide-rule of popular sociological trends. Remember, we are to:

> Test all things; hold fast what is good. Abstain from every form of evil. Now may the God of peace Himself sanctify you completely; and may your whole spirit, soul, and body be preserved blameless at the coming of our Lord Jesus Christ.
>
> *1 Thessalonians 5:21-23*

In this passage of Scripture, there seems to be a connection between abstaining from every form of evil and living in peace, awaiting the return of Jesus Christ. As parents, we must teach our children to live in a state of readiness for our Lord's return. Such an individual would be vigilant and alert, not imprudent or apathetic. Compromising behavior would be considered unwise to those who are looking for Jesus' return.

Whenever our mind tempts us to justify fleshly impulses, we usually ask ourselves, "What's wrong with this thought?" But, filled with the Holy Spirit, we should be asking, "What's right with this thought?"

The same principle that we use to challenge our thinking should be applied to what we hear. Scripture prophesies about a time when people "will turn their ears away from the truth, and be turned aside to fables" (2 Timothy 4:4).

Distractions

Satan is doing all he can to distract children from hearing and embracing the truth. We are cautioned in Scripture to censor what we allow inside our heart and mind. Proverbs 4:23 says, "Keep your heart with all diligence, for out of it spring the issues of life." The eyes and ears of our children are the gateways to their souls.

A godly principle that is true in agriculture is also invaluable in parenting:

> You shall not sow your vineyard with different kinds of seed, lest the yield of the seed which you have sown and the fruit of your vineyard be defiled.
>
> *Deuteronomy 22:9*

Any activity that captures the attention of our children should reinforce the godly principles we are trying to teach them. At the very least, the activities should not contradict these principles!

Deadly or Divine Fruit

Christian parents should eagerly want to ensure that the seeds planted in their child's heart will produce the fruit of the Spirit (Galatians

5:22). Certainly, we don't want to defile that fruit by sowing another kind of seed. A child's ability to face future challenges will depend on the quality of seed germinating in his or her heart.

If your child has been feeding upon Pokémon, and other games that promote self-exalting philosophies, your child's ability to trust in God's power will be diluted. Instead, God instructs us how to guard our hearts:

> Finally, brethren, whatever things are true, whatever things are noble, whatever things are just, whatever things are pure, whatever things are lovely, whatever things are of good report, if there is any virtue and if there is anything praiseworthy, meditate on these things.
>
> *Philippians 4:8*

This Scripture is a valuable passage to teach your child. It contains God's checklist to help your child evaluate what he or she sees and hears. If an activity does not measure up to the qualities mentioned in Philippians 4:8, then it is not worth our time and attention. As we learn to guard our heart, we will enjoy more of God's peace in our life (Philippians 4:9).

Dismissing the Harm

Some Christian parents may claim that Pokémon is only a game.

They believe their child can distinguish between fantasy and reality. However, how can a parent allow their child to role-play behavior that the Bible calls foolish and demonic?

Role-playing and virtual reality games can blur the lines between fantasy and reality. Inflicting headaches, poisoning, paralyzing, and draining the life out of another person or animal can only be called evil and sadistic. It is not the ways of God. He brings life, not death.

Death, destruction, torment and enslavement are schemes orchestrated by Satan. It's his calling card.

As Christian parents, there are many harmless fads in our children's world that we can afford to patiently endure until they pass away. Pokémon may very well be another passing fad, but it cannot be classified as harmless. It teaches a philosophy which contradicts the principles of God's Kingdom and it undermines the very virtues that Christians seek to instill in their children.

Cultivate Discernment

Instead of taking the path of least resistance, we should proactively guide our children. At this time in history, it's too detrimental to take a laissez-faire attitude about parenting. Instead, I would recommend that you use Pokémon as an opportunity to teach your child about spiritual discernment. Show your child how to recognize the enemy's subtle deceptions.

Kids need to know that real Christianity is not an à-la-carte belief system where we pick and choose the parts of God's Word which go down easily. Jesus Christ came to give healing and wholeness to our fractured lives. In so doing, He came to fulfill the Scriptures, not dismiss them.

We must also teach our children not to rationalize sin, merely because it comes wrapped in the guise of a game. None of us should simply "unplug" in such a way that would desensitize our conscience. Our spirit continually receives data, whether the activity is real or fantasy.

Learning to Honor God

Honoring God requires that we recognize and turn from whatever has captured our devotion and adoration. If we love God, we prove our devotion by being obedient to His commandments (John 14:15). Our covenant with Him is one of personal devotion to God. In Him alone lies our true fulfillment.

God's first commandment is: "I am the Lord your God, you shall have no other gods before Me" (Exodus 20:3).

As Christian parents, we must show our children how to keep God first and foremost in their lives. Learning to discern and to make wise choices is an important part of growing up.

Train up
a child
in the way
he should go,
and when he is old
he will not
depart from it.

Chapter Six

How Do We Evict the Monsters?

Karen grew up in a strong Christian home. She invited Jesus Christ into her heart when she was eight. All of her life, she had been a godly child. She attended a strong youth group at a well-respected church. She excelled in all her classes. However, when Karen was a senior in high school, things began to change.

She formed relationships with other teenagers who were poor influences on her. Trying to rescue a friend from smoking marijuana, Karen became addicted to it. Shortly thereafter, she became sexually active. When a counselor probed her as to why she had strayed from God, Karen pointed to her parents' compromises and to a church that felt boring when compared to the enticements of the world.

57

Steps to Freedom

Like Karen, many children and teenagers are faced with unbelievable peer pressure and a global entertainment industry aimed at ensnaring them or liberating them, depending on your point of view. So, what should parents do in relation to Pokémon and other enticements that lure their children away from God?

Step One—Obviously, the first step is prayer. Ask God to help you reach your child's heart. Many parents assume their children will resist them, underestimating the power of the Holy Spirit to influence the child who belongs to Him.

If your child has learned to love the Scriptures and to respect its wisdom and authority, they will usually respond quickly when shown what the Bible has to say on a particular matter. This is especially true if you have first paved the way with prayer.

If your child fights or resists you, a stronghold may exist in their minds. It must be broken. Again, I would recommend two excellent books that provide more information on breaking strongholds: *A Comprehensive Guide to Deliverance and Inner Healing* by John & Mark Sandford and *Healing the Nations* by John Sandford.

Don't simply ban Pokémon from your household without taking time to show your child why it is harmful. Ask what the game teaches about violence. Ask if the source of supernatural power is from God or from Satan. Ask if the game's symbols link it to the occult or to eastern mysticism.

Set aside time to discuss the game—on an age-appropriate level—and show your child Scripture. Then, let God's Word convict their heart. Your child will have a greater ability to stick with his or her convictions when you are absent, if he or she has been convinced from God's Word. Ultimately, your child must learn to think in the spirit, rather than to be governed by sensual thoughts which are tainted by the soul.

Step Two——The second step is to never underestimate the power that you wield through your wallet. If you don't provide the funds for an addiction, it will die. Instead, use the opportunity to teach your child about godly stewardship. Even a young child will understand that if our money belongs to God, then God would not want us to spend His money on something He has declared to be wrong. You may also want to share why you wouldn't buy certain things for yourself, and thereby, model wise decision-making skills.

Step Three——Finally, the third step is to provide positive alternatives to replace whatever you are withholding from your child. Believe it or not, many children would simply prefer the time and attention of their parents over playthings. Often as parents, we are tempted to take the easy way out—allowing television or video games to occupy our children's time. But that's simply a diversion.

Proactive parenting does require more thoughtfulness and

effort, but the rewards are great. We must never lose sight that our goal as parents isn't simply to monitor behavior. Our goal is to cultivate godly character in the hearts of our children.

We are also given these divine instructions:

> Train up a child in the way he should go, and when he is old he will not depart from it.
>
> *Proverbs 22:6*

Standing on Higher Ground

Spiritual battles are won and lost by whomever controls the higher ground. In the battle against the enemy over the souls of our children, it is imperative that we never retreat or relinquish the high place of our parental position.

The game of Pokémon encourages our children to defeat their opponents through deception, psychic energy and violence. But as Christians, we are taught in Scripture to overcome our enemies by blessing and loving them. Scripture also teaches that the fruit of the Spirit—peace, gentleness, goodness, kindness, and self-control—should be obvious to everyone with whom we come in contact.

Your Child's Destiny

God has an incredible and awesome destiny for your child. He created your child with a glorious purpose in mind. But did you know there are circumstances that can prevent your child from walking into his or her destiny? Did you realize that Satan will create circumstances meant to distract and abort your child's destiny?

As parents, we need to become more discerning about various influences that affect our children. The end-time destiny of our children depends on our response.

Come Out of Babylon

Today, demonically inspired pastimes challenge our spiritual beliefs. Violence, anarchy and occult-oriented themes are prevalent in our media. They often mock or misinterpret biblical truths.

I believe that we are living in an age described by the apostle John in Revelation 18. John foretold of a time when the entire world system would be dominated by Satan. Operating an incredibly wicked commercial system, the merchants of the Earth would buy and sell everything from gold and cattle to the very souls of men, women and children (Revelation 18:13). As such, Babylon symbolizes false religion, sorcery, astrology and rebellion. God's judgement on Babylon indicates His hatred for business founded and operated on greed and oppression.

Call To Holiness

As our children are being lured into the mysterious realms of darkness, we need to heed God's prophetic call (Revelation 18:4). We need to come out of Babylon. We need to separate ourselves from the world and all that is false.

As Paul Cain, a mature international prophetic voice, has passionately said:

> This is not a time to sleep. This is not a time to numb our senses with the wine of Babylon... This is the time for soberness... We are on the threshold of the greatest move of God in the history of the world... God wants to visit His people in an unprecedented way. He wants to pour out His Spirit without measure.[14]

Babylon will fall. Come out from her seduction and snares, or you will fall with her and share in her plagues. Instead, keep alert and remain in prayer, so that you may escape all the things that will come to pass (Luke 21:35-36). God has called us to be a people of holiness who are set apart to display His glory (2 Peter 3:11-14).

In our day, God is raising up a new breed of champions. They will live passionately for God. They will have the mind of Christ and will boldly speak forth the Word of God to a lost and dying world. They will pull down enemy strongholds and lay down their lives for the cause of Christ. Their zeal will astound many. They will be Joel's mighty army—trained to walk in obedience, patience and endurance. They will have supernatural strength and great courage, the like of which has never been seen on the Earth (Joel 2:1-22).

Since our children have such an awesome destiny awaiting them, we should walk wisely, "redeeming the time, because the days are evil" (Ephesians 5:16).

> "Now, therefore," says the Lord, "turn to Me with all your heart, with fasting, with weeping and with mourning." So rend your heart and not your garments; return to the Lord your God, for He is gracious and merciful, slow to anger, and of great kindness; and He relents from doing harm.
>
> *Joel 2:12-13*

Training Future Champions

God has given us divine instruction to help us protect our children and our home.

> I will behave wisely in a perfect way...I will walk within my house with a perfect heart. I will set nothing wicked before my eyes...It shall not cling to me. I will not know wickedness...He

who works deceit shall not dwell within my
house; he who tells lies shall not continue in
my presence.

Psalm 101:2-7

Whenever we allow books, television shows and games into our homes that encourage our children to role-play sadistic violence and psychic power, we are allowing the enemy—"he who works deceit"—to dwell in our house. Likewise, whenever we allow materials into our homes that promote evolution and reincarnation, we are permitting the enemy—"he who tells lies"—to remain in our home. However, when we embrace the guidelines found in Scripture and walk in the fear of the Lord, we are entitled to obtain a powerful promise that God has given to parents.

In the fear of the Lord there is strong confi-
dence, and his children will have a place of
refuge.

Proverbs 14:26

Let's build a refuge for our children in these perilous times and train them to become God's champions.

End Notes

1. C. S. Lewis, *The Screwtape Letters* (1961; reprinted, Nashville: Broadman & Holman Publishers, 1996) p. 15.

2. Pokémon Trading Card Game Rules, Version 2 (Renton, WA: Wizards of the Coast, Inc., 1999), p. 2.

3. Ibid., p. 2.

4. Rick Sarlat, "Pokémon Crime Wave Hits Philadelphia: Four Middle School Students Arrested in Attacks," APBnews.com, December 9, 1999.

5. "Psyduck," Pokédex, Pokémon World: The Official Pokémon Website, (electronic document on-line) available from http://www.pokemon.com

6. Howard Chua-Eoan & Tim Larimer, "Pokémania," *Time*, Vol. 154, No. 21., November 22, 1999, p. 84.

7. John Loren Sandford, *Healing the Nations* (Grand Rapids, MI: Chosen Books, 2000) p. 153-154. Used with permission.

8. Debbie Messina, "Playing with Danger? Fantasy Game Debated," The Virginian-Pilot and The Ledger Star, March 17, 1991, p. A6.

9. Berit Kjos, "The Dangers of Role-Playing Games: How Pokémon and Magic Cards Affect the Minds and Values of Children" (an electronic document on-line) available from the website Crossroad.to.

10. Nancy Justice, "The Pokémon Invasion," *Charisma*, February 2000, p. 64.

11. John Loren Sandford & Mark Sandford, *A Comprehensive Guide to Deliverance and Inner Healing* (Grand Rapids, MI: Chosen Books, 1992) p. 308. Used with permission.

12. Ibid, pp. 333-340.

13. Kjos, p. 3. Transcribed from a recorded interview with Cecile DiNozzi in Pound Ridge, New York.

14. Paul Cain, New Years Eve Message (Kansas City: Metro Christian Fellowship, December 31, 1998). Used with permission.

Appendix

Pokémon Descriptions

My purpose in providing this appendix is so that you will have the opportunity to read for yourself the potential damage that can be inflicted by each Pokémon. To research a specific Pocket Monster, simply locate the assigned Pokémon number and read the description provided.

The source of the information was gleaned from numerous fan sites as well as by doing a search under "Pokémon abilities" on the Pokédex–an encyclopedia of information on each Pokémon–which is located on the Pokémon website (www.pokemon.com). As you will see, many responses in this role-playing game involve violent or psychic behaviors.

BULBASAUR (Pokémon #001)

Type: Grass/*Poison*
Evolution: Bulbasaur → Ivysaur *L16* → Venusaur *L32*
Fighting abilities include tackling, growling, whipping, using poison and cutting.

IVYSAUR (Pokémon #002)

Type: Grass/*Poison*
Evolution: Bulbasaur → Ivysaur → Venusaur *L32*
Fighting abilities include growling, whipping, using poison and cutting.

VENUSAUR (Pokémon #003)

Type: Grass/*Poison*
Evolution: Bulbasaur → Ivysaur → Venusaur
Fighting abilities include growling, whipping, using poison and cutting.

CHARMANDER (Pokémon #004)

Type: Fire
Evolution: Charmander → Charmeleon *L16* → Charizard *L36*
Fighting abilities include scratching, growling, burning its victim, mesmerizing its victim with a penetrating stare, slashing and using rage.

CHARMELEON (Pokémon #005)

Type: Fire
Evolution: Charmander → Charmeleon → Charizard *L36*
Fighting abilities include scratching, growling, burning its victim, mesmerizing its victim with a penetrating stare, slashing and using rage.

CHARIZARD (Pokémon #006)

Type: Fire/Flying
Evolution: Charmander → Charmeleon → Charizard
Fighting abilities include scratching, growling, burning its victim, mesmerizing its victim with a penetrating stare, slashing and using rage. This creature spits fire at its opponents.

SQUIRTLE (Pokémon #007)

Type: Water
Evolution: Squirtle → Wartortle *L16* → Blastoise *L36*
Fighting abilities include whipping, biting, bashing and powerfully spraying a foam from its mouth.

WARTORTLE (Pokémon #008)

Type: Water
Evolution: Squirtle → Wartortle → Blastoise *L36*
Fighting abilities include whipping, biting, bashing and stalking its prey.

BLASTOISE (Pokémon #009)

Type: Water
Evolution: Squirtle → Wartortle → Blastoise
Fighting abilities include whipping, biting and bashing. This brutal creature also uses pressurized water jets for high-speed tackles.

CATERPIE (Pokémon #010)

Type: Bug
Evolution: Caterpie → Metapod *L7* → Butterfree *L10*
Fighting abilities include tackling its victim.

METAPOD (Pokémon #011)

Type: Bug
Evolution: Caterpie → Metapod → Butterfree *L10*
No fighting ability. It simply hardens its shell in self-defense. This creature is waiting to evolve into a higher form.

BUTTERFREE (Pokémon #012)

Type: Bug/Flying
Evolution: Caterpie → Metapod → Butterfree
Fighting abilities include causing confusion, using poison, paralyzing its victim, hitting and using psychic powers.

WEEDLE (Pokémon #013)

Type: Bug/*Poison*
Evolution: Weedle → Kakuna *L7* → Beedrill *L10*
Fighting abilities include using poison and stinging its victim.

KAKUNA (Pokémon #014)

Type: Bug/*Poison*
Evolution: Weedle → Kakuna → Beedrill *L10*
No fighting ability. It simply hardens its shell in self-defense.

BEEDRILL (Pokémon #015)

Type: Bug/*Poison*
Evolution: Weedle → Kakuna → Beedrill
Fighting abilities include rage attacks and using poison.

PIDGEY (Pokémon #016)

Type: Normal/Flying
Evolution: Pidgey → Pidgeotto *L18* → Pidgeot *L36*
Fighting abilities include creating blinding storms and using psy-chic powers.

PIDGEOTTO (Pokémon #017)

Type: Normal/Flying
Evolution: Pidgey ➜ Pidgeotto ➜ Pidgeot
Fighting abilities include fiercely pecking its victim, creating blinding storms and using psychic powers.

PIDGEOT (Pokémon #018)

Type: Normal/Flying
Evolution: Pidgey ➜ Pidgeotto ➜ Pidgeot
Fighting abilities include creating blinding storms, stalking its prey and using psychic powers.

RATTATA (Pokémon #019)

Type: Normal
Evolution: Rattata ➜ Raticate *L20*
Fighting abilities include tackling, whipping and biting.

RATICATE (Pokémon #020)

Type: Normal
Evolution: Rattata ➜ Raticate
Fighting abilities include tackling, whipping and biting.

SPEAROW (Pokémon #021)

Type: Flying
Evolution: Spearow ➔ Fearow *L20*
Fighting abilities include pecking, mesmerizing its victim with a
penetrating stare, attacking with rage and using psychic powers.

FEAROW (Pokémon #022)

Type: Normal/Flying
Evolution: Spearow ➔ Fearow
Fighting abilities include pecking, mesmerizing its victim with a
penetrating stare, attacking with rage and using psychic powers.

EKANS (Pokémon #023)

Type: *Poison*
Evolution: Ekans ➔ Arbok *L22*
Fighting abilities include biting, screeching, using poison and mes-
merizing its victim with a penetrating stare.

ARBOK (Pokémon #024)

Type: *Poison*
Evolution: Ekans ➔ Arbok
Fighting abilities include biting, screeching, using poison and mes-
merizing its victim with a penetrating stare.

PIKACHU (Pokémon #025)

Type: Electric
Evolution: Pikachu ➜ Raichu

Fighting abilities include using electric shock and psychic powers. Its electricity could build and cause lightning storms.

RAICHU (Pokémon #026)

Type: Electric
Evolution: Pikachu ➜ Raichu

Fighting abilities include using electric shock with high voltage power.

SANDSHREW (Pokémon #027)

Type: Ground
Evolution: Sandshrew ➜ Sandslash *L22*

Fighting abilities include scratching, slashing, attacking with rage and sending a blinding sandstorm, hitting and using poison.

SANDSLASH (Pokémon #028)

Type: Ground
Evolution: Sandshrew ➜ Sandslash

Fighting abilities include scratching, slashing, attacking with rage, hitting, using poison and sending a blinding sandstorm. When threatened, the creature curls into a spiny ball to attack.

NIDORAN (F) (Pokémon #029)

Type: *Poison*
Evolution: Nidoran (F) ➔ Nidorina *L16* ➔ Nidoqueen *Moon Stone*
Fighting abilities include growling, scratching, biting, whipping,
furiously hitting, kicking and using poison. Its venomous barbs
make this creature dangerous.

NIDORINA (Pokémon #030)

Type: *Poison*
Evolution: Nidoran (F) ➔ Nidorina *L16* ➔ Nidoqueen *Moon Stone*
Fighting abilities include growling, scratching, biting, whipping,
furiously hitting, kicking and using poison. This creature prefers
physical attacks such as clawing and biting.

NIDOQUEEN (Pokémon #031)

Type: *Poison*/Ground
Evolution: Nidoran (F) ➔ Nidorina ➔ Nidoqueen
Fighting abilities include whipping, scratching, tackling, slamming
its body to crush its victim and using poison.

NIDORAN (M) (Pokémon #032)

Type: *Poison*
Evolution: Nidoran (M) ➔ Nidorino *L16* ➔ Nidoking *Moon Stone*
Fighting abilities include kicking, furiously attacking, mesmerizing
its victim with a penetrating stare, stinging and using poison.
This creature secretes powerful venom through its horns.

NIDORINO (Pokémon #033)

Type: *Poison*
Evolution: Nidoran (M) ➔ Nidorino ➔ Nidoking *Moon Stone*
Fighting abilities include furiously hitting, kicking, stinging, mesmerizing its victim with a penetrating stare and using poison.This aggressive monster is quick to attack. Its horn secretes a powerful venom.

NIDOKING (Pokémon #034)

Type: *Poison*/Ground
Evolution: Nidoran (M) ➔ Nidorino ➔ Nidoking
Fighting abilities include tackling, furiously attacking, smashing and breaking its victim's bones and using poison.

CLEFAIRY (Pokémon #035)

Type: Normal
Evolution: Clefairy ➔ Clefable *Moon Stone*
Fighting abilities include hitting, slapping and using psychic powers.

CLEFABLE (Pokémon #036)

Type: Normal
Evolution: Clefairy ➔ Clefable
Fighting abilities include slapping and hiding.

VULPIX (Pokémon #037)

Type: Fire
Evolution: Vulpix ➔ Ninetales *Fire Stone*
Fighting abilities include burning its victim, whipping and using psychic powers.

NINETALES (Pokémon #038)

Type: Fire
Evolution: Vulpix ➔ Ninetales
Fighting abilities include burning its victim, whipping and using psychic energies. This menacing creature can place upon its victim a 1,000-year curse.

JIGGLYPUFF (Pokémon #039)

Type: Normal
Evolution: Jigglypuff ➔ Wigglytuff *Moon Stone*
Fighting abilities include crushing, slapping, hitting and using psychic powers.

WIGGLYTUFF (Pokémon #040)

Type: Normal
Evolution: Jigglypuff ➔ Wigglytuff *Moon Stone*
Fighting abilities include slapping, hitting and using psychic powers. When angered, this monster will suck in air and inflate its size.

ZUBAT (Pokémon #041)

Type: *Poison*/Flying
Evolution: Zubat ➜ Golbat *L22*
Fighting abilities include biting, flying, using ultrasonic waves and various psychic powers.

GOLBAT (Pokémon #042)

Type: *Poison*/Flying
Evolution: Zubat ➜ Golbat
Fighting abilities include biting, hazing, causing confusion, draining energy from its victim and using various psychic powers.

ODDISH (Pokémon #043)

Type: Grass/*Poison*
Evolution: Oddish ➜ Gloom *L21* ➜ Vileplume *Leaf Stone*
Fighting abilities include paralyzing victim, using poison and various psychic powers.

GLOOM (Pokémon #044)

Type: Grass/*Poison*
Evolution: Oddish ➜ Gloom ➜ Vileplume *Leaf Stone*
Fighting abilities include paralyzing its victim, using poison and various psychic powers. Fluid oozes from its mouth to attract prey.

VILEPLUME (Pokémon #045)

Type: Grass/*Poison*
Evolution: Oddish ➜ Gloom ➜ Vileplume
Fighting abilities include paralyzing victims and using poison.

PARAS (Pokémon #046)

Type: Bug/Grass
Evolution: Paras ➜ Parasect *L24*
Fighting abilities include scratching, slashing, paralyzing its victim and using psychic powers.

PARASECT (Pokémon #047)

Type: Bug/Grass
Evolution: Paras ➜ Parasect
Fighting abilities include scratching, slashing, paralyzing its victim and using psychic powers.

VENONAT (Pokémon #048)

Type: Bug/*Poison*
Evolution: Venonat ➜ Venomoth *L31*
Fighting abilities include paralyzing victim, using poison and various psychic abilities.

VENOMOTH (Pokémon #049)

Type: Bug/*Poison*
Evolution: Venonat ➔ Venomoth
Fighting abilities include paralyzing victim, using poison and various psychic abilities. Its dust-like scales are color-coded to indicate the type of poison.

DIGLETT (Pokémon #050)

Type: Ground
Evolution: Diglett ➔ Dugtrio *L26*
Fighting abilities include scratching, slashing, growling and the ability to cause earthquakes.

DUGTRIO (Pokémon #051)

Type: Ground
Evolution: Diglett ➔ Dugtrio
Fighting abilities include scratching, slashing, growling and the ability to cause earthquakes.

MEOWTH (Pokémon #052)

Type: Normal
Evolution: Meowth ➔ Persian *L28*
Fighting abilities include scratching, slashing, growling, screeching, biting and furiously hitting.

PERSIAN (Pokémon #053)

Type: Normal
Evolution: Meowth → Persian

Fighting abilities include scratching, slashing, growling, screeching, biting and furiously hitting. Creature is known for its fickle meanness.

PSYDUCK (Pokémon #054)

Type: Water
Evolution: Psyduck → Golduck *L33*

Fighting abilities include scratching, hitting, causing confusion, mesmerizing its victims with a penetrating stare and using psychic powers.

GOLDUCK (Pokémon #055)

Type: Water
Evolution: Psyduck → Golduck

Fighting abilities include scratching, hitting, causing confusion, mesmerizing its victims with a penetrating stare and using psychic powers.

MANKEY (Pokémon #056)

Type: Fighting
Evolution: Mankey → Primeape *L28*

Fighting abilities include scratching, thrashing, karate, causing confusion, mesmerizing its victims with a penetrating stare and using psychic powers. Like Dr. Jeckle and Mr. Hyde, it can go from being extremely passive to dangerously volatile in seconds.

PRIMEAPE (Pokémon #057)

Type: Fighting
Evolution: Mankey ➔ Primeape

Fighting abilities include scratching, thrashing, karate, causing confusion, mesmerizing its victim with a penetrating stare and using psychic powers. This creature is always furious and tenacious. It stalks its victim until it has been captured.

GROWLITHE (Pokémon #058)

Type: Fire
Evolution: Growlithe ➔ Arcanine *Fire Stone*

Fighting abilities include biting, burning its victim and mesmerizing its victim with a penetrating stare.

ARCANINE (Pokémon #059)

Type: Fire
Evolution: Growlithe ➔ Arcanine

Fighting abilities include roaring, burning its victim and mesmerizing its victim with a penetrating stare.

POLIWAG (Pokémon #060)

Type: Water
Evolution: Poliwag ➔ Poliwhirl *L25* ➔ Poliwrath *Water Stone*

Fighting abilities include slapping, slamming its body against its victim and using psychic powers.

POLIWHIRL (Pokémon #061)

Type: Water
Evolution: Poliwag → Poliwhirl → Poliwrath *Water Stone*
Fighting abilities include slapping, slamming its body against its victim and using psychic powers.

POLIWRATH (Pokémon #062)

Type: Water/Fighting
Evolution: Poliwag → Poliwhirl → Poliwrath
Fighting abilities include slamming its body against its victim and using psychic powers.

ABRA (Pokémon #063)

Type: *Psychic*
Evolution: Abra → Kadabra *L16* → Alakazam *Trade Kadabra*
Fighting abilities include various psychic energies. This creature has the ability to read minds and teleport.

KADABRA (Pokémon # 064)

Type: *Psychic*
Evolution: Abra → Kadabra → Alakazam *Trade Kadabra*
Fighting abilities include various psychic powers such as mind reading, teleporting and the ability to inflict headaches on its victim.

ALAKAZAM (Pokémon #065)

Type: *Psychic*
Evolution: Abra ➔ Kadabra ➔ Alakazam
Fighting abilities include various psychic powers including mind reading, teleporting, and causing confusion.

MACHOP (Pokémon #066)

Type: Fighting
Evolution: Machop ➔ Machoke *L28* ➔ Machamp *Trade Machoke*
Fighting abilities include various martial arts and mesmerizing its victim with a penetrating stare.

MACHOKE (Pokémon #067)

Type: Fighting
Evolution: Machop ➔ Machoke ➔ Machamp *Trade Machoke*
Fighting abilities include various martial arts and mesmerizing its victim with a penetrating stare.

MACHAMP (Pokémon #068)

Type: Fighting
Evolution: Machop ➔ Machoke ➔ Machamp
Fighting abilities include various martial arts, mesmerizing its victim with a penetrating stare and using powerful punches to send its victim over the horizon.

BELLSPROUT (Pokémon #069)

Type: Grass/*Poison*
Evolution: Bellsprout → Weepinbell *L21* → Victreebel
Fighting abilities include whipping, slashing, throwing body slams and using poison.

WEEPINBELL (Pokémon #070)

Type: Grass/*Poison*
Evolution: Bellsprout → Weepinbell *L21* → Victreebel *Leaf Stone*
Fighting abilities include whipping, slashing, paralyzing its victim, throwing body slams and using poison. This creature spits poison and then kills its victim with a spray of acid.

VICTREEBEL (Pokémon #071)

Type: Grass/*Poison*
Evolution: Bellsprout → Weepinbell *L21* → Victreebel *Leaf Stone*
Fighting abilities include holding its victim to make it immobile, attacking several times and using poison.

TENTACOOL (Pokémon #072)

Type: Water/*Poison*
Evolution: Tentacool → Tentacruel *L30*
Fighting abilities include using stinging acid, poison and pummeling its victim with extreme force of water.

TENTACRUEL (Pokémon #073)

Type: Water/*Poison*
Evolution: Tentacool → Tentacruel
Fighting abilities include using stinging acid, poison, immobilizing and pummeling its victim with extreme force of water.

GEODUDE (Pokémon #074)

Type: Rock/Ground
Evolution: Geodude → Graveler *L25* → Golem *Trade Graveler*
Fighting abilities include throwing rocks, causing explosions, tackling and causing earthquakes.

GRAVELER (Pokémon #075)

Type: Rock/Ground
Evolution: Geodude → Graveler *L25* → Golem *Trade Graveler*
Fighting abilities include throwing rocks, causing explosions, tackling and causing earthquakes.

GOLEM (Pokémon #076)

Type: Rock/Ground
Evolution: Geodude → Graveler *L25* → Golem
Fighting abilities include throwing rocks, causing explosions, tackling and causing earthquakes.

PONYTA (Pokémon #077)

Type: Fire
Evolution: Ponyta ➜ Rapidash *L40*

Fighting abilities include burning its victim, stomping, whipping, growling and using psychic powers. This creature can trample anything completely flat in seconds.

RAPIDASH (Pokémon #078)

Type: Fire
Evolution: Ponyta ➜ Rapidash *L40*

Fighting abilities include burning its victim, stomping, whipping, growling and using psychic powers. A very competitive creature, it will chase anything that moves fast.

SLOWPOKE (Pokémon #079)

Type: Water/*Psychic*
Evolution: Slowpoke ➜ Slowbro *L37*

Fighting abilities include growling, head butting and using psychic powers.

SLOWBRO (Pokémon #080)

Type: Water/*Psychic*
Evolution: Slowpoke ➜ Slowbro

Fighting abilities include growling, head butting and using psychic powers.

MAGNEMITE (Pokémon #081)

Type: Electric
Evolution: Magnemite → Magneton *L30*

Fighting abilities include tackling, using electric shocks, screeching and paralyzing its victim. This creature can appear without warning.

MAGNETON (Pokémon #082)

Type: Electric
Evolution: Magnemite → Magneton

Fighting abilities include tackling, using electric shocks, screeching and paralyzing its victim.

FARFETCH'D (Pokémon #083)

Type: Normal/Flying
No Evolution

Fighting abilities include slashing, pecking, mesmerizing its victim with a penetrating stare, furiously attacking and using psychic powers.

DODUO (Pokémon #084)

Type: Normal/Flying
Evolution: Doduo → Dodrio *L31*

Fighting abilities include slashing, pecking, using rage, mesmerizing its victim with a penetrating stare, furiously attacking and using psychic powers.

DODRIO (Pokémon #085)

Type: Normal/Flying
Evolution: Doduo ➜ Dodrio

Fighting abilities include pecking, using rage, mesmerizing its victim with a penetrating stare, furiously attacking and using psychic powers. This creature uses its three brains to execute complex plans; while two heads sleep, one stays awake.

SEEL (Pokémon #086)

Type: Water
Evolution: Seel ➜ Dewgong *L34*

Fighting abilities include growling, head bashing and freezing its victim.

DEWGONG (Pokémon #087)

Type: Water/Ice
Evolution: Seel ➜ Dewgong

Fighting abilities include growling, head bashing and freezing its victim.

GRIMER (Pokémon #088)

Type: *Poison*
Evolution: Grimer ➜ Muk *L38*

Fighting abilities include hitting, screeching and using poison.

MUK (Pokémon #089)

Type: *Poison*
Evolution: Grimer → Muk
Fighting abilities include hitting, screeching and using poison gas. This creature is covered with a thick layer of filthy, vile sludge that is extremely toxic.

SHELLDER (Pokémon #090)

Type: Water
Evolution: Shellder → Cloyster *Water Stone*
Fighting abilities include tackling, using psychic powers, freezing its victim and causing confusion.

CLOYSTER (Pokémon #091)

Type: Water/Ice
Evolution: Shellder → Cloyster
Fighting abilities include tackling, using psychic powers, freezing its victim, causing confusion and attacking in quick volleys.

GASTLY (Pokémon #092)

Type: *Ghost/Poison*
Evolution: Gastly → Haunter *L25* → Gengar *Trade Haunter*
Fighting abilities include eating dreams, hypnosis, causing confusion and using toxic gas and psychic powers.

HAUNTER (Pokémon #093)

Type: *Ghost/Poison*
Evolution: Gastly ➜ Haunter ➜ Gengar *Trade Haunter*
Fighting abilities include eating dreams, hypnosis, causing confusion and paralysis and using psychic powers. This creature is rumored to be from another dimension.

GENGAR (Pokémon #094)

Type: *Ghost/Poison*
Evolution: Gastly ➜ Haunter ➜ Gengar
Fighting abilities include eating dreams, hypnosis, causing confusion, paralysis and using psychic powers. This creature likes to mimic people's shadows and laugh at their fright.

ONIX (Pokémon #095)

Type: Rock/Ground
No Evolution
Fighting abilities include tackling, screeching, binding, throwing rocks, rage and crushing its victim with body slams.

DROWZEE (Pokémon #096)

Type: *Psychic*
Evolution: Drowzee ➜ Hypno *L26*
Fighting abilities include head butting, causing confusion and using various psychic powers such as eating its victim's dreams.

HYPNO (Pokémon #097)

Type: *Psychic*
Evolution: Drowzee ➜ Hypno
Fighting abilities include head butting, causing confusion, using poison and various psychic powers.

KRABBY (Pokémon #098)

Type: Water
Evolution: Krabby ➜ Kingler *L28*
Fighting abilities include crushing its victim, mesmerizing its victim with a penetrating stare, stomping its victim to death and using a vice grip.

KINGLER (Pokémon #099)

Type: Water
Evolution: Krabby ➜ Kingler
Fighting abilities include crushing its victim, mesmerizing its victim with a penetrating stare, stomping its victim to death and using a vice grip. This creature has 10,000 hit points of crushing power.

VOLTORB (Pokémon #100)

Type: Electric
Evolution: Voltorb ➜ Electrode *L30*
Fighting abilities include tackling, causing explosions and shocking people.

ELECTRODE (Pokémon #101)

Type: Electric
Evolution: Voltorb ➜ Electrode
Fighting abilities include tackling, causing explosions and shocking people. It often explodes with little or no provocation.

EXEGGCUTE (Pokémon #102)

Type: Grass
Evolution: Exeggcute ➜ Exeggutor *Stone Leaf*
Fighting abilities include paralysis, poison and using various psychic powers.   When disturbed, these creatures attack in swarms.

EXEGGUTOR (Pokémon #103)

Type: Grass/*Psychic*
Evolution: Exeggcute ➜ Exeggutor
Fighting abilities include stomping and using psychic powers.

CUBONE (Pokémon #104)

Type: Ground
Evolution: Cubone ➜ Marowak *L28*
Fighting abilities include rage attacks, growling, thrashing, mesmerizing its victim with a penetrating stare, and using psychic powers.

MAROWAK (Pokémon #105)

Type: Ground
Evolution: Cubone ➜ Marowak

Fighting abilities include rage attacks, thrashing, growling, mesmerizing its victim with a penetrating stare, and using psychic powers. This creature throws a bone like a boomerang to knock out its targets.

HITMONLEE (Pokémon #106)

Type: Fighting
No Evolution

Fighting abilities include various martial arts and using psychic powers.

HITMONCHAN (Pokémon #107)

Type: Fighting
No Evolution

Fighting abilities include using electric shock, psychic powers, and throwing fire punches in lightning fast volleys that are impossible to see.

LICKITUNG (Pokémon #108)

Type: Normal
No Evolution

Fighting abilities include stomping, screeching, slamming and using psychic energies.

KOFFING (Pokémon #109)

Type: *Poison*
Evolution: Koffing ➔ Weezing *L35*
Fighting abilities include using toxic poison and exploding without warning.

WEEZING (Pokémon #110)

Type: *Poison*
Evolution: Koffing ➔ Weezing *L35*
Fighting abilities include using toxic poison and exploding without warning.

RHYHORN (Pokémon #111)

Type: Ground/Rock
Evolution: Rhyhorn ➔ Rhydon *L42*
Fighting abilities include stomping, attacking with fury, stabbing, whipping and mesmerizing its victim with a penetrating stare.

RHYDON (Pokémon #112)

Type: Ground/Rock
Evolution: Rhyhorn ➔ Rhydon
Fighting abilities include stomping, attacking with fury, stabbing, whipping and mesmerizing its victim with a penetrating stare.

CHANSEY (Pokémon #113)

Type: Normal
No Evolution

Fighting abilities include slapping, mesmerizing its victim with a penetrating stare and using psychic powers.

TANGELA (Pokémon #114)

Type: Grass
No Evolution

Fighting abilities include slamming, paralyzing its victim and using poison.

KANGASKHAN (Pokémon #115)

Type: Normal
No Evolution

Fighting abilities include rage, biting, punching, whipping and using psychic powers.

HORSEA (Pokémon #116)

Type: Water
Evolution: Horsea ➔ Seadra *L32*

Fighting abilities include using psychic powers and mesmerizing its victim with a penetrating stare.

SEADRA (Pokémon #117)

Type: Water
Evolution: Horsea ➜ Seadra
Fighting abilities include using psychic powers and mesmerizing its victim with a penetrating stare.

GOLDEEN (Pokémon #118)

Type: Water
Evolution: Goldeen ➜ Seaking *L33*
Fighting abilities include pecking, whipping, attacking with fury, stabbing and using psychic powers.

SEAKING (Pokémon #119)

Type: Water
Evolution: Goldeen ➜ Seaking
Fighting abilities include pecking, whipping, attacking with fury, stabbing and using psychic powers.

STARYU (Pokémon #120)

Type: Water
Evolution: Staryu ➜ Starmie *Water Stone*
Fighting abilities include tackling and using psychic energies.

STARMIE (Pokémon #121)

Type: Water/*Psychic*
Evolution: Staryu ➜ Starmie

Fighting abilities include using psychic powers. This creature's central core glows with seven colors.

MR. MIME (Pokémon #122)

Type: *Psychic*
No Evolution

Fighting abilities include using various psychic powers. If interrupted, this creature will slap the offender.

SCYTHER (Pokémon #123)

Type: Bug/Flying
No Evolution

Fighting abilities include mesmerizing its victim with a penetrating stare, slashing and using psychic powers. This creature can create the illusion that there is more than one.

JYNX (Pokémon #124)

Type: Ice/*Psychic*
No Evolution

Fighting abilities include punching, slapping and using psychic powers. This creature has a female appearance and seductively moves its hips.

ELECTABUZZ (Pokémon #125)

Type: Electric
No Evolution

Fighting abilities include shocking its victim, attacking, screeching, mesmerizing its victim with a penetrating stare and paralyzing its victim. This creature can also cause major blackouts in cities.

MAGMAR (Pokémon #126)

Type: Fire
No Evolution

Fighting abilities include burning its victim, using poison and various psychic powers.

PINSIR (Pokémon #127)

Type: Bug
No Evolution

Fighting abilities include cutting off the head of its victim, using a vice grip, slashing and using swords. If it fails to crush the victim, this creature will swing around and toss it hard.

TAUROS (Pokémon #128)

Type: Normal
No Evolution

Fighting abilities include stomping its victim, whipping, rage attacks and mesmerizing its victim with a penetrating stare.

MAGIKARP (Pokémon #129)

Type: Water
Evolution: Marikarp ➔ Gyarados
Fighting abilities include tackling and splashing.

GYARADOS (Pokémon #130)

Type: Water/Flying
Evolution: Magikarp ➔ Gyarados
Fighting abilities include biting, using dragon-like rage, using intimidating stares and psychic abilities. Huge and vicious, this creature is capable of destroying entire cities in a rage.

LAPRAS (Pokémon #131)

Type: Water/Ice
No Evolution
Fighting abilities include growling, body slams, creating confusion, freezing its victim and using various psychic powers.

DITTO (Pokémon #132)

Type: Normal
No Evolution
Fighting abilities include using various psychic powers. By duplicating its opponent's genetic code, this creature can instantly transform itself into the enemy.

EEVEE (Pokémon #133)

Type: Normal
Evolution: Eevee ➔ Vaporean *Waterstone* ➔ Jolteon *Thunder Stone* ➔ Flareon *Fire Stone*
Fighting abilities include attacking, biting and whipping.

VAPOREON (Pokémon #134)

Type: Water
Evolution: Eevee ➔ Vaporeon
Fighting abilities include biting, attacking, whipping, using poison and freezing its victim.

JOLTEON (Pokémon #135)

Type: Electric
Evolution: Eevee ➔ Jolteon
Fighting abilities include attacking, kicking, using electric shock, causing paralysis and using various psychic powers.

FLAREON (Pokémon #136)

Type:Fire
Evolution: Eevee ➔ Flareon
Fighting abilities include burning its victim, attacking, whipping, biting, using rage and mesmerizing its victim with a penetrating stare.

PORYGON (Pokémon #137)

Type: Normal
No Evolution
Fighting abilities include attacking swiftly and using psychic powers. This creature is capable of moving freely in cyberspace.

OMANYTE (Pokémon #138)

Type: Rock/Water
Evolution: Omanyte → Omastar *L40*
Fighting abilities include leering and using cannon-like sprays of water.

OMASTAR (Pokémon #139)

Type: Rock/Water
Evolution: Omanyte → Omastar
Fighting abilities include spiking with a horn, leering and using cannon-like sprays of water.

KABUTO (Pokémon #140)

Type: Rock/Water
Evolution: Kabuto → Kabutops
Fighting abilities include scratching, slashing, leering and using forceful sprays of water.

KABUTOPS (Pokémon #141)

Type: Rock/Water
Evolution: Kabuto ➜ Kabutops
Fighting abilities include scratching, slashing, leering and draining its victim's body fluids.

AERODACTYL (Pokémon #142)

Type: Rock/Flying
No Evolution
Fighting abilities include biting, attacking with its appendages and using psychic powers. This vicious creature attacks its victim's throat with its serrated fangs.

SNORLAX (Pokémon #143)

Type: Normal
No Evolution
Fighting abilities include head butting, body slams, and using psychic powers.

ARTICUNO (Pokémon #144)

Type: Ice/Flying
No Evolution
Fighting abilities include pecking, freezing its victim and using psychic powers.

ZAPDOS (Pokémon #145)

Type: Electric/Flying
No Evolution

Fighting abilities include pecking, using electric shock, paralyzing its victim and using psychic powers.

MOLTRES (Pokémon #146)

Type: Fire/Flying
No Evolution

Fighting abilities include pecking, leering, burning its victim and using psychic powers.

DRATINI (Pokémon #147)

Type: Dragon
Evolution: Dratini → Dragonair *L30* → Dragonite *L55*

Fighting abilities include leering, using electric shock to paralyze, slamming, dragon rage, and using various psychic powers.

DRAGONAIR (Pokémon #148)

Type: Dragon
Evolution: Dratini → Dragonair → Dragonite *L55*

Fighting abilities include slamming, using electric shock, leering, dragon rage, and using psychic powers. This creature has the ability to change the weather.

DRAGONITE (Pokémon #149)

Type: Dragon/Flying
Evolution: Dratini → Dragonair → Dragonite

Fighting abilities include slamming, using electric shock, leering, dragon rage, and using psychic powers. This creature's intelligence matches that of humans.

MEWTWO (Pokémon #150)

Type: *Psychic*
No Evolution

Fighting abilities include various psychic powers. This creature was created after years of horrific gene splicing and DNA engineering experiments.

MEW (Pokémon #151)

Type: *Psychic*
No Evolution

Fighting abilities include punching, pounding and using various psychic powers. This creature is so rare that it is said to be a mirage. Only a few people worldwide have seen it.

Order Form

▶ Order online at our secure site: **www.streamsministries.com**
▶ Call toll-free in the continental U.S.: **1-888-441-8080**
▶ Fax orders: **817-536-7710**
▶ Postal orders: **Streams Publications, P.O. Box 101808, Fort Worth, TX 76185-1808 USA**

Quantity	*Title*	*Price*
_____	**Buying & Selling the Souls of Our Children**	$11.00
_____	**Needless Casualties of War**	$13.00

Subtotal _____

Shipping and Handling _____

Total this Order _____

(Please print clearly)

Name_____

Street Address_____

City_____ State/Prov._____ ZIP/Postal Code_____

Country_____ Daytime Phone_____

E-mail_____

Method of Payment

___ Check or Money Order (Make check payable to Streams Ministries)

___ Visa   ___ MasterCard

Credit Card No. _____-_____-_____-_____ Expiration Date___ /___

Signature_____

(Credit card orders cannot be processed without signature)

Shipping and Handling Charges: $4.00 for first book and $2.00 for each additional book. • For AK, HI, PR, USVI, Canada or Mexico, please double the shipping charges. • All international orders must be paid by credit card only. Please specify surface or airmail shipping. The cost will be added to your charges.

Order Form

◗ Order online at our secure site: **www.streamsministries.com**
◗ Call toll-free in the continental U.S.: **1-888-441-8080**
◗ Fax orders: **817-536-7710**
◗ Postal orders: **Streams Publications, P.O. Box 101808, Fort Worth, TX 76185-1808 USA**

Quantity	Title	Price
_____	**Buying & Selling the Souls of Our Children**	$11.00
_____	**Needless Casualties of War**	$13.00

Subtotal _____

Shipping and Handling _____

Total this Order _____

(Please print clearly)

Name_____

Street Address_____

City_____ State/Prov._____ ZIP/Postal Code_____

Country_____ Daytime Phone_____

E-mail_____

Method of Payment

____ Check or Money Order (Make check payable to Streams Ministries)

____ Visa   ____ MasterCard

Credit Card No. _____-_____-_____-_____ Expiration Date____ /____

Signature _____

(Credit card orders cannot be processed without signature)

Shipping and Handling Charges: $4.00 for first book and $2.00 for each additional book. • For AK, HI, PR, USVI, Canada or Mexico, please double the shipping charges. • All international orders must be paid by credit card only. Please specify surface or airmail shipping. The cost will be added to your charges.